I0412415

The month of June, from the illuminated manuscript *Les Trés Riches Heures du duc de Berry*

*The Story of a Special Day*
*Volume 176*

# June

# 24

175th day of the year
(176th in leap years)
190 days remaining
until the end of the year.

by Michael Dobson

# Timespinner
# Press

For more information about the series, about us, or about your special day, please email us at editor@timespinnerpress.com.

Look for other volumes in *The Story of a Special Day,* coming often. See www.timespinnerpress.com for details and for the most recent information.

**For the definition of "O.S.," "CE," and "BCE" used with some dates , see the section "On Names and Dates."**

# Table of Contents

**Cover:** The cover photograph shows US Air Force C-47s and US Navy R4D aircraft unloading supplies at Templehof Airport during the Berlin Airlift — for the *Event of the Day*.

President Grover Cleveland, by Eastman Johnson (1891)

# June 24 Quotations

"The cynic is one who never sees a good quality in a man and never fails to see a bad one."
— *Henry Ward Beecher, clergyman, reformer, and author, born June 24, 1813*

"**Egotist, n.** A person of low taste, more interested in himself than me."
— *from* The Devil's Dictionary *by Ambrose Bierce, born June 24, 1842*

"Mathematics is one of the essential emanations of the human spirit, a thing to be valued in and for itself, like art or poetry."
— *Oswald Veblen, mathematician, born June 24, 1880*

"A champion is someone who gets up when he can't."
— *Jack Dempsey, boxer, born June 24, 1895*

"What is the use of being elected or re-elected unless you stand for something?"
— *Grover Cleveland, US president, died June 24, 1908*

"Space isn't remote at all. It's only an hour's drive away if your car could go straight upwards."
— *Fred Hoyle, astronomer, born June 24, 1915*

Berliners watching an incoming C-54 during the Berlin Airlift

# The Berlin Blockade Begins

In the aftermath of World War II, the victorious Allied powers agreed to divide conquered Germany into four occupation zones, intended to be temporary. One zone each was controlled by the United States, the United Kingdom, France, and the Soviet Union. Berlin, the capital, was also divided into four sectors, even though it was located about 100 miles inside the Soviet sector.

In June 1945, Soviet leader Joseph Stalin informed leaders of the German Communist Party of his intention to undermine the Western powers and reunite Germany as a communist nation under Soviet control. One key element in his plan was to take full control of Berlin.

Unfortunately for the three Western Allies, there was no formal agreement requiring the Soviets to allow railway and road access to Berlin. Initially, the Soviets merely restricted cargo access to a single rail line and three limited air corridors. In 1946, the Soviets stopped shipment of agricultural goods from Eastern Germany, and in response the US commander stopped shipment of industrial goods from Western Germany.

Competition between the Western Allies and the Soviet Union for control of Berlin intensified. The importance of this conflict was made clear by Soviet

Foreign Minister Vyacheslav Molotov. "What happens to Berlin, happens to Germany; what happens to Germany, happens to Europe."

Tensions steadily escalated. The Soviets began stopping British and American trains to Berlin to check passenger identifications. The Western Allies agreed to unify their three zones and to extend the Marshall Plan to Germany. The Soviets then began searching all trains and trucks to prevent any cargo leaving Berlin without their permission. Fearing the worst, the Western Allies began stockpiling goods in Berlin. The Soviets started harassing incoming flights, and in April 1948 a Soviet fighter collided with a British passenger airplane, killing everyone aboard.

Because of massive inflation, the Western Allies introduced a new Deutche Mark currency, competing with the Soviet Ostmark currency. The Soviets began military maneuvers outside the city.

On June 24, 1948, the escalating problems turned into a crisis when the Soviets imposed a complete blockade of the non-Soviet sectors of Berlin. Food, electricity, and cargo were blocked. Because of postwar drawdowns, the Americans and British were greatly outnumbered, and the Soviets believed that the Western Allies would quickly give in to pressure.

This turned out not to be the case. Although no treaty guaranteed Western access to Berlin by road or rail, there was a written agreement allowing air traffic. To survive, Berlin needed a minimum of 5,000 tons of food, coal, and other supplies a day. Unfortunately, the Western Allies had fewer than 200 cargo aircraft available for the job, capable of no more than 750 tons each day.

US Occupation Commander General Lucius Clay, along with his British counterpart General Sir Brian Robertson, agreed that an airlift was Berlin's only hope, and even then it would be a dangerous and difficult operation. Berliners would be on short rations and suffer hardship, but Berlin Mayor Ernst Reuter said that his citizens would nevertheless support the effort.

On the first day, only 80 tons of cargo were flown to Berlin, and the initial operation was plagued with logistical problems. Direct responsibility for the airlift was transferred to the deputy commander of the Military Air Transport Service (MATS), Major General William Tunner, who had led the resupply effort for Chinese forces, known as "the Hump." Soon, an aircraft was landing at Berlin's Templehof Airfield every three minutes. Berlin's citizens volunteered to unload the planes.

Two months into the airlift, the Western Allies were flying more than 1,500 flights a day, delivering more than 4,500 tons of cargo. Although Berliners were on short rations, this was enough to survive.

Morale was vital. Airlift pilot Gail Halvorsen began dropping chocolate bars attached to handkerchief parachutes for children who came to watch the planes fly in. He became known as "Uncle Wiggly" for wiggling his wings to let the children know he was overhead. Other pilots joined in, and over 23 tons of candy were dropped for the children of Berlin.

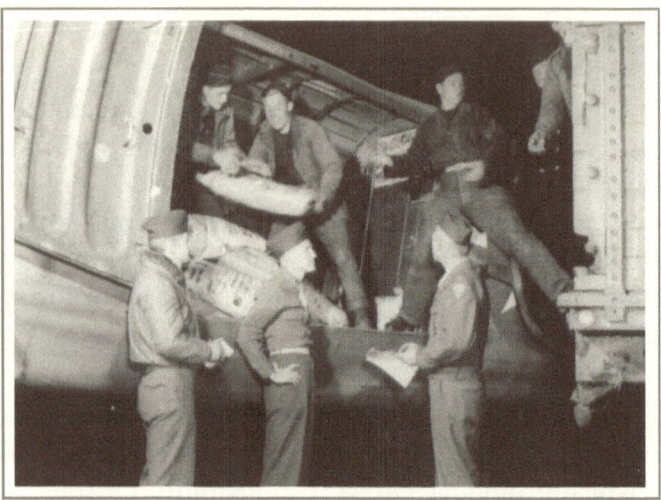

Soldiers and civilians in Frankfurt load a cargo flight for Berlin

In an attempt to recover on the propaganda front, the Soviets offered free food to Berliners who would cross into East Berlin to register their ration cards, but few accepted the offer. Meanwhile, the Soviets attempted to harass incoming aircraft short of acts of war, but were unsuccessful. In September, Communist-led mobs attempted a coup against the government of the western sectors, but a crowd of over 500,000 Germans protested successfully to stop the takeover. This resulted in increased Allied determination not to ignore the citizens of Berlin.

The airlift continued into winter, when the need for coal dramatically increased the tonnage required to support the beleaguered city. The runways at Templehof and Gatow Airports began to fail under the daily operations. Monthly tonnage grew from 171,000 tons to over 230,000 tons.

By April 1949 it was clear that the Soviet efforts to take Berlin had failed, and after negotiations, the blockade was lifted one minute after midnight on May 12, 1949. Unsure of Soviet intentions, the airlift continued until July, stockpiling three months of goods in case of another blockade.

Over 275,000 flights took place during the Berlin Airlift, flying a total of 92 million miles, the distance from the Earth to the Sun. At its height, one plane reached Berlin every 30 seconds, delivering a total of over 2.5 million tons of cargo. There were 101 fatalities, mostly from non-flying accidents, and there were 25 crashes. The total cost of the airlift has been estimated at between US$224 and over $500 million, the equivalent of between $2.2 and $5 billion in today's currency.

Berlin children playing a game about the Berlin Airlift

Earliest known depiction of the Battle of Bannockburn, 1440s

# June 24 Holidays and Celebrations

## Bannockburn Day (Scotland)

The Battle of Bannockburn (*Blàr Allt nam Bànag* in Scottish Gaelic), a major Scottish victory in the First War of Scottish Independence, took place on June 23 and 24, 1314. Although the English army was more than twice as large, the Scots, led by Robert the Bruce, were triumphant, and the English fled the field in a rout. The Scots celebrate Bannockburn Day each June 24 in honor of this victory.

## Battle of Carabobo Day (Venezuela)

The Battle of Carabobo, which took place on June 24, 1821, resulted in the defeat of the Spanish by Venezuelan forces under the leadership of General Simón Bolívar, and the independence of Venezuela. It is also celebrated in that country as Army Day.

## Dia do Cabocio (Amazonas, Brazil)

In Brazilian Portuguese, a *cabocio* is a person of mixed indigenous Brazilian and European ancestry. The Brazilian state of Amazonas celebrates each June 24 as the Day of the Cabocio.

Battle of Carabobo, by Martin Tovar y Tovar

## Discovery Day (Newfoundland and Labrador)

Discovery Day in the Canadian provinces of Newfoundland and Labrador commemorates the anniversary of John Cabot's discovery of Newfoundland on June 24, 1497. It is celebrated on the Monday nearest June 24.

## Feast of Raḥmat (Bahá'í Faith)

In the Bahá'í faith, each of their months is celebrated by a feast. The month of Rahmat (Mercy) begin on June 24 each year, although calendar differences sometimes move the celebration to another day.

## National Pralines Day (United States)

In the United States, almost every day of the year is dedicated to a particular food. Sponsored by manufacturers, retailers, farmers, or simply fans, these days are often proclaimed by the President, Congress, state governors, or mayors.

June 24 is National Pralines Day. Pralines are a type of candy. American pralines are a combination of syrup and pecans, hazelnuts, or almonds, combined with milk or cream, resulting in a candy resembling fudge. In France, pralines are a combination of almonds and caramelized sugar; Belgian pralines have a chocolate shell with a softer filling of nuts, sugar, syrup, and cream.

## Nativity of St. John the Baptist (Roman Catholic Church and various European nations))

The birth of John the Baptist, the prophet who foretold the coming of Jesus according to the New Testament, is celebrated in many countries on June 24. This observance has many different names, including Enyovden (Bulgaria), Jaanipäev (Estonia), Jónsmessa (Iceland), Midsummer Day (England) and Sânziane (Carpathian Mountains, Romania). The latter event is actually a pagan celebration of the summer solstice, named for legendary fairies in the region.

## Youth Day (Ukraine)

Many countries celebrate Youth Day, dedicated to the young people of that country, although different days are honored in different countries. In the Ukraine, Youth Day is June 24.

## Christian Feast Days

In *Western Christianity*, Saint Maria Guadalupe Garcia Zavala is commemorated on June 24.

In *Eastern Orthodox Christianity*, it is the commemoration of Saint Anthony of Dymsk, Saint Nicetas of Remesian, Saint John of Yaransk, Saint Michael of Tyvr, as well as the Synaxis of the Righteous Zechariah and Elizabeth, parents of John the Baptist. (These are celebrated on July 7 by "Old Calendarists.")

## Other Holidays

Some holidays are simply made up by individuals, companies, or other organizations, and whether they become widely adopted depends on whether people choose to celebrate them. Here are some opportunities to celebrate on June 24.

June 24 is:

- Celebration of the Senses
- Countrymans Day (Peru)
- Flying Saucer Day
- International Fairy Day
- Macau Day (China)
- Swim a Lap Day

# What Happened on June 24?

### 1509 – Coronation of Henry VIII and Catherine of Aragon

In 1503, when he was only 11 years old, the future King Henry VIII of England was betrothed to Catherine of Aragon, youngest daughter of King Ferdinand and Queen Isabella. Henry became king upon his father's death in 1509, married Catherine a month later, and on June 24, the official coronation ceremony took place. When Henry VIII began an affair with Anne Boleyn some fifteen years later, he attempted to have the marriage annulled, resulting in the creation of the Church of England.

Henry VIII and Catherine of Aragon, by B. Trell

## 1717 – First Masonic Grand Lodge

The Premier Grand Lodge of England, the first Masonic Grand Lodge, was founded on June 24, 1717. In 1813, it united with the Ancient Grand Lodge of England to create the United Grand Lodge of England

## 1812 – Napoleon Invades Russia

On June 24, 1812, Napoleon's Grande Armée crossed the Neman (Nieman) River into Russia, beginning what is known in France as the Campagne de Russie and in Russia as the Patriotic War of 1812 (Отечественная война 1812 года). Five months of bitter fighting resulted in a decisive Russian victory and the end of Napoleon's reputation as invincible. Of a French force of 685,000, only 120,000 survived; the Russians lost 210,000.

The French Army crosses the Neman River (Auguste Raffet)

## 1880 – First Performance of "O Canada"

The song that became the Canadian national anthem, "O Canada," was first performed on June 24, 1880, at a Saint-Jean-Baptiste Day banquet in Quebec City.

## 1947 – First Modern UFO Sighting

On June 24, 1947, private pilot Kenneth Arnold claimed to have seen nine unidentified flying objects (UFOs) flying past Mount Rainier, Washington, at speeds in excess of 1,200 miles per hour. This gained nationwide press coverage and is considered to be the first UFO sighting of the modern era. (Unexplained aerial phenomena have been noted since at least 240 BCE.) The term "flying saucer" came from Arnold's description.

## 1949 – First TV Western

On June 24, 1949, the NBC television network premiered its first western series, *Hopalong Cassidy*, based on the popular film series starring William Boyd. The series was an immense hit, and spun off merchandise including the first lunchbox with a licensed image.

"Lord Kitchener Wants You" recruiting poster, Alfred Leete, 1914
Herbert Kitchener, 1st Earl Kitchener, born June 24, 1850

# Who Was Born on June 24?

## Business

### Roy O. Disney (June 24, 1893 – December 20, 1971)

Roy O. Disney was the older brother of Walt Disney, and along with Walt, co-founded Walt Disney Productions in 1923 and became the company's first CEO. He oversaw construction of Walt Disney World after the death of his brother in 1966.

### Gustavus Franklin Swift (June 24, 1839 – March 29, 1903)

Founder of the Swift meat-packing empire, Gustavus Swift developed the first ice-cooled railroad car and pioneered the use of animal by-products in such products as soap, glue, fertilizer, and medical products. His work ushered in the "era of cheap beef." He was named to the American National Business Hall of Fame in 2002.

### Thomas Blanchard (June 24, 1788 – April 16, 1864)

American inventor Thomas Blanchard developed the assembly line method of mass production as well as the idea of interchangeable parts. He invented America's first "horseless carriage," a steam-powered automobile. In his lifetime, he earned more than 25 patents for his inventions.

### Éleuthère Irénée du Pont de Nemours (June 24, 1771 – October 31, 1834)

E.I. du Pont was a French-American chemist and industrialist who founded the gunpowder manufacturer, E. I. du Pont de Nemours and Company. His descendants, the Du Pont family, have been one of America's richest and most prominent families since the 19th century.

## Crime

### Walter E. Ellis (June 24, 1960 — December 1, 2013)

Known as the "Milwaukee North Side Strangler," Ellis was sentenced to seven consecutive life sentences without parole.

### Charles Whitman (June 24, 1941 – August 1, 1966)

University of Texas student and mass murderer Charles Whitman, known as the "Texas Tower Sniper," killed 16 and wounded 32 in a shooting spree before being shot and killed by police officers.

## Exploration

### Ellison Onizuka (June 24, 1946 – January 28, 1986)

Hawaiian-born astronaut Ellison Onizuka was the first Asian American and the first person of Japanese ancestry to reach space. He died in the Space Shuttle *Challenger* accident in 1986.

# Film and Television

## Mindy Kaling (June 24, 1979 – )

Vera Mindy Chokalingam, known professionally as Mindy Kaling, created the sitcom *The Mindy Project*, in which she also starred, and appeared on the sitcom *The Office*.

## Sherry Stringfield (June 24, 1967 – )

Sherry Stringfield received three Emmy nominations for playing Dr. Susan Lewis on the medical drama *ER*.

## Tom "Tiny" Lister, Jr. (June 24, 1958 — )

Tiny Lister is known for his roles in the *Friday* series, *The Fifth Element*, and many other films. He also had a brief career as a WWF wrestler.

## Nancy Allen (June 24, 1950 –)

Nancy Allen first became known for her supporting role in the 1976 film *Carrie*, directed by Brian De Palma, whom she later married. She appeared in several of De Palma's films including *Dressed to Kill* and *Blow Out,* as well as films directed by Steven Spielberg and Robert Zemeckis.

## Peter Weller (June 24, 1947 – )

Peter Weller is best known for his performance in the title role of *RoboCop*, as well as for roles in such films as *Buckaroo Banzai, Mighty Aphrodite*, and such TV series as *24*.

## Clarissa Dickson Wright (June 24, 1947 – March 15, 2014)

British television chef Clarissa Dickson Wright co-starred in the *Two Fat Ladies* cooking show and played the gamekeeper in the sitcom *Absolutely Fabulous*. She was an accredited cricket umpire and one of only two women to become a Guild Butcher of the Worshipful Company of Butchers.

## Michelle Lee (June 24, 1942 –  )

Actress and singer Michelle Lee is best known for her role as Karen in the prime-time soap opera *Knots Landing*, in which she was nominated for an Emmy. She also received two Tony Award nominations for her Broadway roles.

## Al Molinaro (June 24, 1919 –  )

Al Molinaro is best known for playing Al Delvecchio, owner of Arnold's on the television series *Happy Days* and its spinoff *Joanie Loves Chachi*, and as Murray the Cop in *The Odd Couple*.

# Letters

## Mercedes Lackey (June 24, 1950 –  )

Fantasy writer Mercedes Lackey is best known for the Valdemar novels.

## Lawrence Block (June 24, 1938 –  )

Mystery writer Lawrence Block has won numerous awards and was named a Grand Master of the Mystery Writers of America in 1994.

Al Molinaro as Murray the Cop

### Ernesto Sabato (June 24, 1911 – April 30, 2011)

Argentine writer and physicist Ernesto Sabato received numerous international awards for his novels, including the French Legion of Honour and the Miguel de Cervantes Prize. He presided over the commission that investigated the forced disappearances during the Dirty War in Argentina.

### Ambrose Bierce (June 24, 1842 – unknown, circa 1914)

Ambrose Bierce is best remembered for *The Devil's Dictionary*, a satirical lexicon, and for his short story "An Occurrence at Owl Creek Bridge." A critic, editor, and reporter, he vanished while reporting on the Mexican Revolution, where he was rumored to be traveling with rebel troops.

## Military and Espionage

### Pearl Witherington (June 24, 1914 – February 24, 2008)

French born British special operations executive (SOE) agent Pearl Witherington led underground networks in France during World War II that played an important role in tying down German forces during the D-Day lands. The Nazis put a ƒ1,000,000 price on her head. Her wartime tales were compiled into a book, *Code Name Pauline*, and she has been cited as the inspiration for the book and film *Charlotte Gray*.

Ambrose Bierce

### Herbert Kitchener, 1st Earl Kitchener (June 24, 1850 – June 5, 1916)

Herbert Kitchener was given the title Lord Kitchener of Khartoum for his victory in the Battle of Omdurman. He commanded the British Army in India and served as British Consul-General for Egypt. As Secretary of State for War, he organized the largest volunteer army ever assembled to fight in World War I. His famous recruiting poster, "Lord Kitchener Wants You," is the model of many similar posters used worldwide.

# Music

### Jeff Cease (June 24, 1967 –  )

Jeff Cease was the lead guitarist of the blues rock band The Black Crowes from 1988 to 1991.

### Curt Smith (June 24, 1961 –  )

Musician Curt Smith is best known for forming the band Tears for Fears and has also recorded numerous solo albums.

### Mick Fleetwood (June 24, 1947 –  )

Drummer Mick Fleetwood co-founded the rock band Fleetwood Mac, which was inducted into the Rock and Roll Hall of Fame in 1998.

Mick Fleetwood (Photo: Joe Bielawa)

## Jeff Beck (June 24, 1944 – )

Rock guitarist Jeff Beck is known for his work with The Yardbirds and The Jeff Beck Group. He has been inducted twice into the Rock and Roll Hall of Fame, once for The Yardbirds and once as a solo artist.

Jeff Beck (Photo: Craig ONeal)

## Phil Harris (June 24, 1904 – August 11, 1995)

Singer and bandleader Phil Harris is best remembered today for his role as Baloo in the Walt Disney animated film The Jungle Book, along with other animation voices. He was the music director and a regular performer on the Jack Benny radio show along with his wife, Alice Faye.

Phil Harris (right) with Alice Faye

# Politics and Government

## Ralph Reed (June 24, 1961 – )

Conservative political activist Ralph Reed is best known as the first executive director of the Christian Coalition.

## Robert Reich (June 24, 1946 – )

Political economist and author Robert Reich was Secretary of Labor under US President Bill Clinton. *Time* Magazine named him one of the ten best Cabinet members of the 20th century and the *Wall Street Journal* cited him as one of the "Most Influential Business Thinkers."

## George Pataki (June 24, 1945 – )

George Pataki was Governor of New York for three terms, one of only three Republican governors of the state elected since 1923.

# Religion

## Henry Ward Beecher (June 24, 1813 – March 8, 1887)

Congregationalist minister Henry Ward Beecher was famous for his support for the abolition of slavery. His sister, Harriet Beecher Stowe, wrote the famous novel *Uncle Tom's Cabin*. In 1872, he was accused of having an affair with the wife of a former associate, who sued him for adultery in what became one of the most infamous and widely reported trials of the 19th century, known as the "Beecher-Tilton Scandal." The trial resulted in a hung jury. A monument to Beecher can be seen in Cadman Plaza, Brooklyn, New York.

Henry Ward Beecher and Harriet Beecher Stowe

## Saint John of Capistrano (June 24, 1386 – October 23, 1456)

Known as the "Soldier Saint," Saint John of Capistrano was a Italian Franciscan friar, known as a theologian and inquisitor. At the age of 70, he led a crusade against the Ottoman Empire at the siege of Belgrade, for which he is considered the patron saint of Hungary, as well as the patron saint of military chaplains and jurists. He was also known for his anti-semitism and for inciting violence against Jews. The famous Mission San Juan Capistrano in California, known for the annual "return of the swallows" is named for him.

Saint John of Capistrano, by Thaler Tamas

# Science and Mathematics

### Carolyn Shoemaker (June 24, 1929 – )

Astronomer Carolyn Shoemaker is known as the co-discoverer of Comet Shoemaker-Levy 9, along with her husband Eugene. She held the record for most comets discovered by an individual, having found 32 comets and over 300 asteroids.

### Martin Perl (June 24, 1927 – September 30, 2014)

Martin Perl won the 1995 Nobel Prize in Physics for his discovery of the tau lepton.

### Fred Hoyle (June 24, 1915 – August 20, 2001)

Astronomer Fred Hoyle was noted for his theory of stellar nucleosynthesis and for his controversial positions on many scientific matters, including his rejection of the "Big Bang Theory," which, ironically, he named. He was also known as a science fiction writer, and wrote the television series (and later book) *A for Andromeda*.

### Victor Hess (June 24, 1883 – December 17, 1964)

Victor Hess won the 1936 Nobel Prize in Physics for the discovery of cosmic rays.

## Oswald Veblen (June 24, 1880 – August 10, 1960)

Mathematician Oswald Veblen's work is used in atomic physics and the theory of relativity. He is known for the first rigorous proof of the Jordan curve theorem, the Veblen-Young Theorem, and Veblen ordinals. He helped develop the first modern computing machines, including the ENIAC. He was the nephew of noted economist Thorstein Veblen.

# Sports

## Gary Suter (June 24, 1964 –  )

Ice hockey defenseman Gary Suter played over 1,000 games in the NHL, and was named to the United States Hockey Hall of Fame in 2011. He won a silver medal in hockey at the 2002 Winter Olympics.

## Preki (June 24, 1963 –  )

A member of the American National Soccer Hall of Fame, Serbian-American Predrag Radosavljević represented the US at the 1998 FIFA World Cup.

## Sam Jones (June 24, 1933 –  )

Basketball shooting guard Sam Jones was named to the Naismith Memorial Basketball Hall of Fame in 1984.

### Billy Casper (June 24, 1931 – February 7, 2015)

Golfer Billy Casper was twice named PGA Player of the Year and won five Vardon Trophies for the lowest seasonal scoring average on the PGA Tour. He was inducted into the World Golf Hall of Fame in 1978.

### Brian Bevan (June 24, 1924 – June 3, 1991)

Rugby player Brian Bevan is the only person ever inducted into both the Australian Rugby League Hall of Fame and the British Rugby League Hall of Fame.

### Chuck Taylor (June 24, 1901 – June 23, 1969)

Basketball player Chuck Taylor (right) is best remembered for his promotion of the the Converse Chuck Taylor All-Stars basketball sneaker, one of the first and the most successful basketball shoe in history, as well as the first official sneaker of the US armed forces. He also invented the "stitchless" basketball. He was elected to the Naismith Memorial Basketball Hall of Fame for his contributions to the sport.

## Jack Dempsey (June 24, 1895 – May 31, 1983)

Boxing icon Jack Dempsey, known as "the Manassa Mauler," was World Heavyweight Champion from 1919 to 1926, and was the first boxer to set the financial record of a $1 million gate. The Associated Press voted him the greatest fighter of the last half century in 1950, and he was elected to the International Boxing Hall of Fame in 1954.

Jack Dempsey

Portrait of Lucrezia Borgia, by Dosso Dossi
Lucrezia Borgia died June 24, 1519

# Who Died on June 24?

## Animals

### Lonesome George (circa 1910 — June 24, 2012)

Tortoise Lonesome George was the last known member of his sub-species, *Chelonoidis nigra abingdonii,* and considered the rarest creature in the world in his later life. He was a symbol of conservation efforts in the Galápagos Islands and elsewhere. He died of old age at the Charles Darwin Research Station on Santa Cruz Island in the Galápagos, where he was kept for many years.

Lonesome George (Photo: Mike Weston)

# Crime

### Patsy Ramsey (December 29, 1956 — June 24, 2006)

Former Miss West Virginia Patsy Ramsey was the mother of child beauty pageant contestant JonBenét Ramsey, whose murder at the age of six was a national obsession.

# Film and Television

### Eli Wallach (December 7, 1915 — June 24, 2014)

Character actor Eli Wallach's many roles include his screen debut in the 1956 black comedy *Baby Doll*, Calvera in *The Magnificent Seven*, Tuco in *The Good, the Bad, and the Ugly*, Don Altobello in *The Godfather Part III*, and Cotton in *The Two Jakes*.

### Paul Winchell (December 21, 1922 — June 24, 2005)

Ventriloquist Paul Winchell hosted his own variety show, featuring his dummies Jerry Mahoney and Knucklehead Smiff. In addition to sitcom guest appearances, Winchell was also a voice artist whose characters included Tigger (*Winnie the Pooh*), Dick Dastardly (*Wacky Races*), and Gargamel (*The Smurfs*).

Winchell, who had studied medicine in college, was also an inventor of medical devices, earning over 30 patents, including an early artificial heart co-developed with Dr. Henry Heimlich, creator of the Heimlich Maneuver.

Paul Winchell (center) with Jerry Mahoney (left) and
Knucklehead Smiff (right)

## David Tomlinson (May 7, 1917 — June 24, 2000)

English actor David Tomlinson is best remembered
as George Banks in the 1964 Walt Disney film *Mary
Poppins*.

David Tomlinson as George Banks in *Mary Poppins* (1964)

## Jackie Gleason (February 26, 1916 — June 24, 1987)

Comedian and actor Jackie Gleason is best remembered for his role as Ralph Kramden in the sitcom *The Honeymooners*. He received an Oscar nomination for Best Supporting Actor for his role as legendary pool player Minnesota Fats in the 1961 film *The Hustler*.

Jackie Gleason (left) with Art Carney and Audrey Meadows in *The Honeymooners* (1965)

# Letters

## Edward de Vere, 17th Earl of Oxford (April 12, 1550 — June 24, 1604)

English nobleman Edward de Vere (see page 42) was a patron of the arts, a poet, and at different times a court favorite. Known to be reckless and temperamental, he never achieved any roles of high responsibility. He was the ward of Queen Elizabeth I, but was exiled from her court after getting one of her maids of honor pregnant. During his lifetime, he lost all his inheritance and lived his remaining years on a small annuity from the Queen.

Although Shakespearean scholar generally dismiss the theory and no hard evidence for it is known to exist, there is a persistent claim that de Vere was the actual author of the plays and poems attributed to William Shakespeare.

# Military and Espionage

## Susan Ahn Cuddy (January 16, 1915 — June 24, 2015)

Korean-American Susan Ahn Cuddy became the first Asian-American woman to join the US Navy, doing so at the height of anti-Asian sentiment during World War II, and became the first female aerial gunnery officer in the Navy, reaching the rank of Lieutenant.

Edward de Vere, Earl of Oxford (artist unknown)

## Vera Atkins (June 16, 1908 — June 24, 2000)

Romanian-born British Special Operations Executive (SOE) officer Vera Atkins recruited and deployed British agents in occupied France. After the war, she conducted searches for agents who had disappeared in enemy territory, interrogating Nazi officials and testifying as a prosecution witness in war crimes trials. She located 117 of the 118 missing agents.

Her story has been told in several documentaries and films, and she is one of the women who may have been the basis for Miss Moneypenny in the *James Bond* novels by Ian Fleming, who was himself a Naval Intelligence officer during the war.

# Music

### Carlos Gardel (December 11, 1890 — June 24, 1935)

French-Argentine singer-songwriter Carlos Gardel (right) is considered the "King of Tango" and the most prominent figure in the history of that dance. He died in an airplane crash at the height of his career, and is mourned by many as a tragic hero.

# Politics and Government

### Grover Cleveland (March 18, 1837 — June 24, 1908)

Grover Cleveland was the 22nd and 24th President of the United States, the only president to have served two non-consecutive terms. He won the popular vote to be the 23rd president, but lost in the Electoral College, the third time in U.S. history that a presidential candidate won the popular vote but lost the election.

Cleveland was accused of having fathered an illegitimate child, leading to the anti-Cleveland slogan, "Ma, Ma, where's my Pa?" to which Cleveland's supporters replied, "Gone to the White House, Ha! Ha! Ha!"

Anti-Cleveland political cartoon by Frank Beard (1884)

## Lucrezia Borgia (April 18, 1480 — June 24, 1519)

Lucrezia Borgia's name has been associated with all matter of evildoing, including poisoning, incest, and murder, although there is no historical basis for these claims. She is supposed to have a hollow ring in which she carried poison. Numerous books, plays, operas, films, and television shows have been made about Lucrezia and her three brothers, including the Showtime series *The Borgias*, and the play by Victor Hugo (later turned into the opera by Felice Romani), *Lucrezia Borgia*.

The historical Lucrezia was the daughter of Pope Alexander VI and one of his many mistresses. The Borgia family was politically important, wealthy, and titled. Lucrezia was both a duchess and a princess of different lands. As a result, her family (including the Pope) made arranged marriages for her. She was married three times and had rumored affairs; she had at least seven known children. The family's often ruthless politics and intrigues are used as examples in Machiavelli's *The Prince*.

# Science and Education

## Marva Collins (August 31, 1936 — June 24, 2015)

Educator Marva Collins's work with impoverished youth in Chicago was featured on the *60 Minutes* news program, leading to the 1981 docudrama *The Marva Collins Story*, in which she was played by Cicely Tyson.

## Willy Ley (October 2, 1906 — June 24, 1969)

German-American science writer Willy Ley helped popularize the idea of rocketry and spaceflight in both countries beginning in the 1920s. He left Germany when the Nazis came to power. In the US, he wrote a number of popular science books in the 1950s and 1960s. He died one month before the first Moon landing; a lunar crater is named in his honor.

Left to right: Aviation medicine expert Dr. Hans Haber, Dr. Wernher von Braun, and Willy Ley

# Sports

## Walter Browne (January 10, 1949 — June 24, 2015)

Walter Browne won the US Chess Championship six times, and was named to the US Chess Hall of Fame in 2003. He also earned more than $250,000 as a professional poker player.

## Olga Kotelko (March 2, 1919 — June 24, 2014)

Canadian track and field athlete Olga Kotelko did not begin her career until the age of 77, and began competing in the World Association of Veteran Athletes, where she set two world records in the W80 category. In her 90s, she broke world records in her age category in the hammer throw and the 100 meter race. She won over 750 gold medals and held every track and field world record she attempted for her age group, for which she is considered one of the world's greatest athletes.

## "Fabulous" Jerry Fargo (June 26, 1930 — June 24, 2013)

Professional wrestler Jerry Fargo, known as "The Fabulous One," held 45 tag team championships in his career and was named to the Professional Wrestling Hall of Fame in 2014.

*June,* by Hans Thoma

# June:
# The Sixth Month

*And what is so rare as a day in June?*
*Then, if ever, come perfect days;*
*Then Heaven tries earth if it be in tune,*
*And over it softly her warm ear lays.*

— *"An April Day," Henry Wadsworth Longfellow*

In the Julian and Gregorian calendars, June is the sixth month of the year. It's one of the four months that have only 30 days. No months start on the same day of the week as June, an oddity shared only by May. However, June ends on the same day of the week as March in both common and leap years.

In the Northern Hemisphere, June is the month with the longest daylight hours; in the Southern Hemisphere, it's the one with the shortest, equivalent to December. The meteorological summer begins June 21 (the Summer Solstice) in the Northern Hemisphere; the meteorological winter begins on the same day in the Southern Hemisphere (the Winter Solstice).

The English name of June takes its name from the Latin *Iunius*. The poet Ovid gives two theories for the origin of the name. The first is that June is named for the Roman goddess Juno, wife of Jupiter and queen of the gods. The second is that the name comes from the Latin word *iuniores* ("younger ones"), and that the previous month of May comes from maiores ("elders")

As the early Roman calendar started its new year in March, June was originally the fourth month of the year. It's uncertain when the Romans switched the new year to January, but it may have been as late as 153 BCE.

# June in Other Cultures

The month of June has different names in different languages. Some nations use calendars other than the Gregorian, and their months may overlap with June. In lunar-based calendars, such as Islam, months move through the seasons. Still, many languages often have a word for *June* itself.

**Albanian:** Qershor

**Arabic (Egyptian, Sudanese, Moroccan):** يونيو (*yūniyū*)

**Arabic (Levantine):** حزيران(*ḥuzayrān*)

**Arabic (Libyan):** الصيف (*al-sayf*)

**Arabic (Algerian):** جوان (*Juwān*)

**Azerbaijani:** İyun

**Basque:** Ekain

**Bulgarian:** юни (*juni*)

**Chinese:** 六月 (Cantonese: *luhkyuht*; Mandarin: *liùyuè*; Taiwanese: *lak-goeh*)

**Corsican:** Chjugnu

**Czech:** červen

**Finnish:** Kesäkuu

**French:** Juin

**German, Norwegian:** Juni

**Greek:** Ιούνιος (*Ioúnios*)

**Hebrew:** יוני (*yûnî*)

**Hindi:** जून (*jūn*)

**Hungarian:** Június

**Irish (Gaelic):** Meitheamh mí an Mheithimh

**Italian:** Giugno

**Japanese (traditional calendar):** 六月 (*rokugatsu*); 水無月 (*minaduki*)

**Korean**: 유월 (*yuweol*)

**Lithuanian:** Birželis

**Maori:** Pipiri

**Old English**: Sēremōnaþ

**Polish**: Czerwiec

**Russian:** июнь (*ijun'*)

**Sesotho:** Phupjane

**Spanish**: Junio

**Swedish, Swahili:** Juni

**Thai:** Mithunayon

**Vietnamese:** 腑嶅 (tháng sáu)

**Welsh:** Mehefin

# June Brides and Other Sayings and Superstitions

June is the most popular month for weddings, followed by August. There are a number of sayings and superstitions about June brides and June weddings.

"A June bride is joyful, jubilant, and jolly well jovial."

"A June bride will be impetuous, and generous."

"Married in the month of roses (June), life will be one long honeymoon."

"Marry when June roses grow, over land and sea you'll go."

"When you marry in June, you'll be a bride all your life." (from the song *June Bride*.)

Why such an emphasis on June? Some say it's in honor of Juno, the goddess of marriage. Others suggest it's because back in Medieval days, people would usually have their (yes) annual bath in May, so they'd still be relatively fresh by June. This may also explain the custom of the bridal bouquet.

According to superstition, May is the most unlucky month for marriages, but in ancient Rome the "inauspicious" period ran from May 15 to June 15. The high priestess of Jupiter told the poet Ovid to delay his daughter's wedding until after that date.

There are also some June proverbs for farmers.

"A calm June puts the farmer in tune."

"June damp and warm, does the farmer no harm."

# June Symbols

**Birthstone**  Pearl, moonstone, or alexandrite.

Pearl

Moonstone

Michael Dobson

Alexandrite

**Birth Flowers** Rose and Honeysuckle

*Roses*, by Vincent van Gogh

Honeysuckle

# June Events

## Honorary Months

Presidents, Congresses, and nations around the world issue proclamations recognizing particular months to honor certain causes. These events generally fall in June, though honorary months do come and go. Holidays established by states and nonprofit organizations are listed if verified. If not otherwise specified, all months are US.

- Adopt a Cat Month
- **African-American Music Appreciation Month**
- Bicycle Month (May 25 to June 25) (Canada)
- Caribbean American Heritage Month
- Children's Awareness Month
- Crop over (Barbados), celebrated until the first Monday in August.

Sarah Vaughn

- Dairy Alternative Month
- Fireworks Safety Month
- Gay and Lesbian Pride Month (US)
- Georgia Blueberry Month
- Great Outdoors Month (US)

- International Surf Music Month
- Men's Health Education and Awareness Month
- National Accordion Awareness Month
- National Camping Month
- National Rivers Month
- National Safety Month
- National Smile Month (UK)
- National Oceans Month (United States)
- Season of Emancipation (April 14 to August 23) (Barbados)
- Women's Golf Month
- World Naked Bike Ride Month (northern hemisphere)

## Moveable and Multi-Day Events

Some events take place over a specific week or time period. Start and finish dates may vary from year to year. Some events occur on different days each year (such as "fourth Saturday of a month"). The following events sometimes occur on June 24.

### A Saturday
- Queen's Official Birthday (United Kingdom) (precise week varies)

### Monday before Father's Day in the United States
- International Men's Health Week: (Begins on the Monday before Father's Day, ends on Father's Day (United States)

### Third Sunday
- Father's Day (United States)

**Friday between June 19–25**

- Midsummer (Sweden)

**Saturday between June 20–25**

- Finnish Flag Day
- Juhannus (Finland)
- National Famine Commemoration Day
- National Famine Commemoration Day (Ireland)

**Saturday nearest Summer Solstice**

- Pixie Day (Ottery St. Mary, England)

**Last Saturday**

- Armed Forces Day (United Kingdom)

**Last Sunday**

- Mother's Day (Kenya)

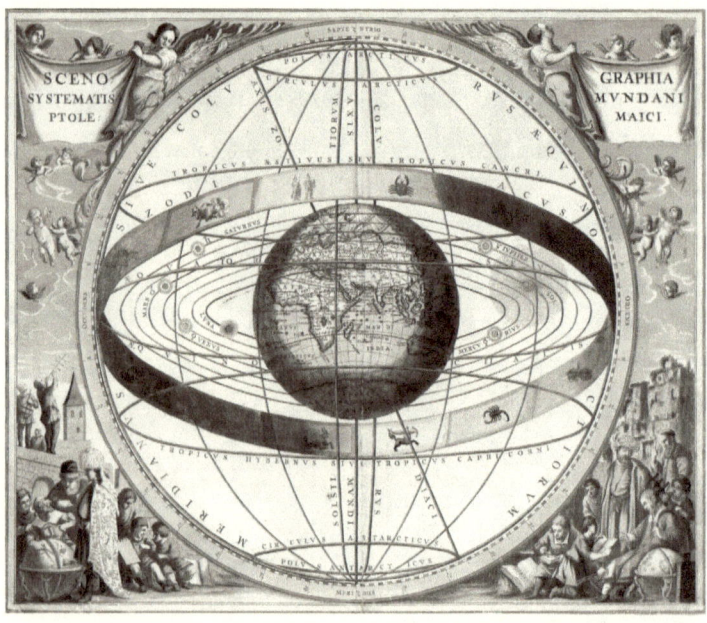

*Scenography of the Ptolemaic Cosmography,* by Johannes van Loon, based on Andreas Cellarius's *Harmonia Macrocosmica,* 1660

# June Zodiac Signs

From the perspective of someone on Earth, the Sun appears to move through the sky throughout the year, along a path astronomers call the *ecliptic plane*. The ecliptic plane is divided into twelve constellations, known as the zodiac, based on traditionally observed patterns of stars. On your birthday, you can't see your constellation, because it's in the daytime sky.

The zodiac was first developed by Babylonian astronomers about 2,500 years ago. Because they were unaware that the Earth wobbles like a spinning top (known as *precession*), they didn't make allowance for the fact that the Sun's path through the zodiac changes over time.

That means there are now two sets of dates for your birth sign. The *tropical dates* are the original Babylonian dates; the *sidereal dates* tell you where the Sun actually appears as it moves along its annual path.

For June 24, the tropical sign is Cancer and the sidereal sign is Gemini.

# Gemini

**Tropical** May 22 to June 21
**Sidereal** June 16 to July 15

According to Greek mythology, Leda, wife of the King of Sparta, gave birth to Helen of Troy and Clytemnestra. The god Zeus, disguised as a swan, seduced her after she had already lain with her husband on the same night. This resulted in two eggs, which hatched to become the twins Castor and Pollux. Castor's father was the King of Sparta, but Pollux was the son of Zeus and therefore immortal. When Castor died, Pollux shared his immortality, so that they could divide their time between Hades and Olympus. They were enshrined in the Zodiac as the constellation Gemini, the Twins.

In astrology, Gemini is an air sign, ruled by Mercury, compatible with Libra, Aquarius, and Aries. Geminis are supposed to be communicative, flexible, intellectual, and curious, but prone to fickleness and easily distracted.

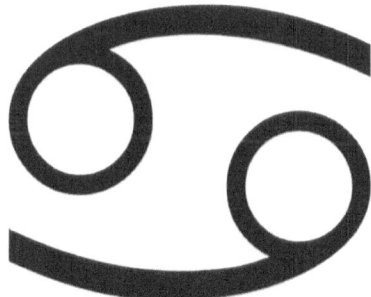

# Cancer

**Tropical** June 22 to July 22
**Sidereal** July 16 to August 15

In Greek mythology, Cancer (the Crab) is connected to the legend of Hercules. Hera, wife of Zeus, had sworn to kill Hercules, so when he was battling the many-headed Hydra, Hera sent a crab to snap at his toes. Hercules killed the crab by stomping on it. Hera rewarded the crab for serving her by placing it in the sky as a constellation.

In astrology, Cancer is a water sign, ruled by the Moon. (Because of its association with the disease, some astrology columns use "Moon Children" in place of Cancer.) Those born under this sign are supposed to be compatible with Taurus, Scorpio, and Virgo. Like their namesake crab, those born under the sign of Cancer retreat into their shell when threatened, and can be a bit crabby at times. However, they are extremely loving and caring, dedicated to protecting their loved ones, and value security and respect for the past.

Illustration by Edward Penfield

# What Day of the Week is June 24?

On what day of the week does June 24 fall?

Surprisingly, this isn't an easy question. Because the calendar year is 365 days long (366 in leap years), it doesn't divide evenly by the seven days of the week.

Also, the Earth goes around the Sun in about 365-1/4 days, so a calendar tends to drift over time. That's why the same date falls on different weekdays in different years.

This is made even more complicated by a change in calendars that took place in 1582. Our modern calendar has its roots in ancient Rome, in a calendar reform conducted by Julius Caesar. Caesar commissioned mathematicians to attack the problem, and they came up with the idea of leap years, and thus standardized the calendar for centuries to come. This was called the Julian calendar.

Over time, however, the small errors in Caesar's calculation compounded. That's why Pope Gregory XIII commissioned the Gregorian calendar, used in most of the world today. Some countries converted in 1582, when the calendar was first developed; some converted later; other still haven't changed.

Gregorian and Julian aren't the only types of calendars. The Hebrew year, the Islamic year, and many other calendars are used in different parts of the world and among different people.

You can convert Gregorian dates to other calendars, including the Hebrew calendar, the Islamic calendar, and even the Mayan calendar by visiting the Fourmilab Calendar Converter at http://www.fourmilab.ch/documents/calendar/.

Chinese calendar systems are quite complex and have changed several times; a full discussion is far beyond the scope of this book. If you're interested, you can find information here: http://www.hermetic.ch/cal_stud/chinese_cal.htm.

# On Names and Dates

Historians use "CE" (Common Era) and "BCE" (Before the Common Era) instead of the more common "AD" (Anno Domini, or Year of Our Lord) and "BC" (Before Christ), reflecting the fact that the year-numbering system established by the Gregorian calendar is used throughout the world in many countries not culturally Christian.

The CE/BCE designation dates back to at least 1708, and has been adopted as a standard by the United Nations and the Universal Postal Union. Because this series of books covers events and people of all nations and cultures, we use the CE/BCE terms.

The abbreviation "O.S." ("Old Style") on some dates refers to the fact that the Russian Empire did not switch from the Julian to the Gregorian calendar at the same time as the rest of Europe, and therefore some figures and events have two dates.

Also, in the Julian calendar in England in the 16th century, the year began on March 25 rather than January 1. To avoid confusion with Gregorian dates, dates between January and March were often written using both years.

People and events whose original names are not in the Western alphabet have their native names (where possible) in the appropriate script shown in parenthesis. If you are using an e-reader to access an electronic version of this book, all characters don't always display on all devices.

A 50-year brass perpetual calendar.

Cartoon by John T. McCutcheon

# Copyright, Credit, and Contact

## Follow Us

Our blog Dobson's Improbable History (http://
improbhistory.blogspot.com) features short articles on events
and people associated with each day, and updates several
times each week. You can also get a daily "What Happened
In History" message and all the latest Timespinner Press
news by following us on Facebook at https://
www.facebook.com/TimespinnerPress. Our Twitter feed
@SidewiseThinker links you to all our News of the Day.

## Contact Us

Find an error or a format problem? Want information about
the series, about us, or about when the volume for your
special day might be available? Please email us at
editor@timespinnerpress.com. (We also take requests if your
special day isn't yet complete. Please give us at least six
weeks' notice if possible.)

## Sources

We owe a great debt to Wikipedia, which is our first stop for
research. We attempt to make independent confirmation of
all important dates and facts through a variety of other
sources. Other sources we frequently use include the Library
of Congress; "on this day" listings from *Encyclopedia
Britannica*, the *New York Times,* and the BBC; Omniglot for the

names of months in other languages; *Chase's Calendar of Events;* and, of course, the always essential Google.

All art and photographs are either in the public domain, used under a Creative Commons license, or with a "fair use" justification, and most frequently come from Wikimedia Commons and the Library of Congress Prints and Photographs Division.

Attribution is provided where possible, or as requested by the copyright owner, or when there is particular historical significance, listed below. For information about any particular illustration or photograph, please contact us.

# Credits

- The cover photograph of aircraft unloading at Templehof Airport during the Berlin Airlift is from the collection of the US Navy Museum of Naval Aviation (2000.043.012) and the National Museum of the US Air Force (050426-F-1234P-008), and was taken either in 1948 or 1949. It is in the public domain as a work created by an employee of the US federal government or a member of its military as part of that person's official duties.
- The illustration of the month of June used on the back cover and as the frontispiece is from the French Gothic illuminated manuscript *Les Très Riches Heures du duc de Berry* by the Limbourg Brothers, Jean Colombe, and an intermediate painter whose name is lost to history.
- The official Presidential portrait of Grover Cleveland by Eastman Johnson was painted in 1891. As a work created by a contract employee of the US federal government, it is in the public domain.
- The 1948 photograph of children watching a C-54 landing at Berlin Templehof Airport is in the public domain as a work created by an employee of the US federal government or a member of its military as part of that person's official duties.
- The 1949 photograph of loading an airplane in Frankfurt is from the German Federal Archives (Bundesarchiv Bild

146-1985-064-02A), and is used here under CC BY-SA 3.0 Germany.

- The 1948 photograph of children playing "Luftbrücke" is in the public domain as a work created by an employee of the US federal government or a member of its military as part of that person's official duties.

- The depiction of the Battle of Bannockburn is from a 1440s manuscript of Walter Bower's *Scotichchronon*, and is in the public domain because its copyright has expired. The original can be found at Corpus Christi College, Cambridge.

- The detail from a 1887 mural of the Battle of Carabobo is by Martin Tovar y Tovar is in the public domain because its copyright has expired. The mural is located in the Palacio Federa Legislativo, Caracas, Venezuela.

- The 19th century portrait of Henry VIII and Catherine of Aragon is by B. Treil. It is in the public domain because its copyright has expired.

- The 19th century engraving of the French Army crossing the Nieman River is by Auguste Raffet, and is in the public domain because its copyright has expired.

- The "Lord Kitchener Wants You" recruitment poster was created by Alfred Leete and first published in 1914 in the *London Opinion*. It is in the public domain because its copyright has expired.

- The 1974 ABC promotional photo of Al Molinaro is in the public domain because it was published in the United States between 1923 and 1977 and without a copyright notice. Traditionally, publicity photographs are not copyrighted because they are intended for general public use.

- The photograph of Ambrose Bierce originally appeared in *The Letters of Ambrose Bierce*, edited by Bertha Clark Pope and published in 1922. It is in the public domain because its copyright has expired.

- The April 2013 photograph of Mick Fleetwood in concert was taken by Joe Bielawa. It is used here under CC BY-SA 2.0. It has been cropped for use in this book.

- The May 2011 photograph of Jeff Beck in concert was taken by Craig ONeal. It is used here under CC BY-SA 2.0. It has been cropped for use in this book.

- The 1950 MCA promotional photo of Alice Faye and Phil Harris is in the public domain because it was published in the United States between 1923 and 1977 and without a copyright notice. Traditionally, publicity photographs are not copyrighted because they are intended for general public use.

- The photograph of Henry Ward Beecher and Harriet Beecher Stowe was taken between 1852 and 1855 by Gurney and Sons, and can be found in the collection of the Bowdoin College Museum of Art. It is in the public domain because its copyright has expired.

- The painting of Saint John of Capistrano (*Kapisztrán Szent János festménye, Pannonhalma*) is by Thaler Tamas, and is used here under CC BY-SA 3.0.

- The 1921 photograph of Chuck Taylor is in the public domain because it was first published prior to 1923.

- The 1927 picture of Jack Dempsey autographed to Raoul Paoli was taken by Alexander Dreyfoos of Apeda Studio before 1927. It is in the public domain because it was published in the United States between 1923 and 1963 and although there may or may not have been a copyright notice, the copyright was not renewed.

- The portrait believed to be of Lucrezia Borgia was painted by Dosso Dossi around 1518. It is in the public domain because its copyright has expired. The painting is in the collection of the National Gallery of Victoria, Melbourne, Australia.

- The 2006 photograph of the tortoise Lonesome George was taken by Mike Weston and is used here under CC BY-SA 2.0.

- The 1958 ABC promotional photo from *The Paul Winchell Show* is in the public domain because it was published in the United States between 1923 and 1977 and without a copyright notice. Traditionally, publicity photographs are not copyrighted because they are intended for general public use.

- The screenshot of David Tomlinson is from the trailer for the 1964 Walt Disney film *Mary Poppins*. Although the film itself is copyrighted, the trailer is in the public domain because it was first published in the United States between 1923 and 1977 without a copyright notice. Traditionally, movie trailers are not copyrighted because they are intended for general public use.

- The 1965 CBS promotional photo from *The Honeymooners* is in the public domain because it was published in the United States between 1923 and 1977 and without a copyright notice. Traditionally, publicity photographs are not copyrighted because they are intended for general public use.

- The painting of Edward de Vere, 17th Earl of Oxford, was painted sometime after 1575 by an unknown artist. It is in the public domain because its copyright has expired.

- The 1933 portrait of Carlos Gardel is by José Maria Silva, and is in the collection of the Archivo General de la Nación. This file has been placed in the public domain according Uruguayan law 9.739, law 17.616, and its subsequent amendments

- The 1884 political cartoon of Grover Cleveland by Frank Beard was originally published in *The Judge* magazine. It is part of the Library of Congress Print and Picture Collection. It is in the public domain because its copyright has expired.

- The photograph "Dr. Wernher von Braun (center), then Chief of the Guided Missile Development Division at Redstone Arsenal, Alabama, discusses a "bottle suit" model with Dr. Heinz Haber (left), an expert on aviation medicine, and Willy Ley, a science writer on rocketry and space exploration," was taken by a NASA photographer on July 1, 1954 (Photo ID: MSFC-9605274). It is in the public domain as a work created by an agency of the US federal government.

- The painting *Juni* is from the calendar book *Festkalender* by Hans Thoma. It is in the pubic domain because its copyright has expired.

- The photo of a pearl necklace is by "Anna reg," taken from Wikimedia Commons and used here under CC BY-SA 3.0.

- The photograph of a Brazilian moonstone is by Didier Descouens, taken from Wikimedia Commons and used here under CC BY-SA 4.0.

- The photograph of alexandrite under ultraviolet light is by Parent Géry, taken from Wikimedia Commons and used here because the creator has dedicated the rights to the public domain under CC0 1.0.

- The painting *Roses* by Vincent Van Gogh can be found in the collection of the National Gallery of Art, Washington, DC. The image is in the public domain because its copyright has expired.

- The illustration of honeysuckle originally appeared in the book *American Homes and Gardens*, published by Munn & Co., New York, in 1905. It is in the public domain because its copyright has expired. The image was taken from Flickr's The Commons.

- The 1946 photograph of Sarah Vaughn was taken by William P. Gottlieb, and is part of the William P. Gottlieb Collection of jazz photographs at the Library of Congress. In accordance with the wishes of Gottlieb, the photographs in the collection entered into the public domain in 2010.

- The celestial sphere is from *Scenography of the Ptolemaic Cosmography*, by Johannes van Loon, based on Andreas Cellarius's *Harmonia Macrocosmica*, 1660. It is in the public domain because its copyright has expired.

- The 1906 automobile calendar is by Edward Penfield, and is in the collection of the Library of Congress Prints and Photographs Division. It is in the public domain because its copyright has expired.

- The 50-year perpetual calendar photograph is in the public domain.

- The cartoon by John T. McCutcheon is from his 1905 collection *The Mysterious Stranger and Other Cartoons by John T. McCutcheon*. It is in the public domain because its copyright has expired.

## License Description and Terms

Aside from material purely in the public domain, photographs and other material in this book are used under specific licenses permitting free use, usually with an attribution requirement. For full text and terms of these licenses, click or enter the appropriate links below. If you believe there is an error in the copyright status or attribution of any of these images, please email us.

Timespinner
Press

# Other Books from Timespinner Press

### *The Story of a Special Day*
*Michael Dobson*

A series of (eventually) 366 volumes covering everything that happened on your special day! Events, births, deaths, quotes, holidays, and much more. It's like a birthday card they'll never throw away!

US$7.95 print / US$2.99 ebook.

### *From Plassey to Pakistan*
*Humayun Mirza*

The history of British Colonial India and the formation of Pakistan from the unique perspective of the son of Pakistan's first president and last of the royal line of Bengal, Bihar, and Orissa!

US$27.95 print

### *A Whole New Navy: America's War in the Pacific*
*Miles Durr*

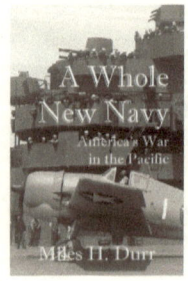

The most comprehensive and detailed description of America's naval war in the Pacific ever—every battle, every ship, every task force and every task group from Pearl Harbor through the Japanese surrender!

US$29.95 print